Anonymous

How to catch Trout

Anonymous

How to catch Trout

ISBN/EAN: 9783337141363

Printed in Europe, USA, Canada, Australia, Japan

Cover: Foto ©Lupo / pixelio.de

More available books at **www.hansebooks.com**

HOW TO CATCH TROUT.

OPINIONS OF THE PRESS.

"A delightful little book, and one of great value to anglers. . . . The work is sound in the essential doctrines of the craft."—*Scotsman*.

"The advice given by the 'Three Anglers,' whose combined wisdom is bound within the covers of this book, is always sound."—*Field*.

"Gives a vast amount of information to beginners, and in which skilled anglers may find hints and suggestions worth their attention."—*Scottish People*.

"As perfect a compendium of the subject as can be compressed within 83 pages of easily read matter."—*Scotch Waters*.

"This little work will be of some service in teaching the young idea, and may even be found to contain a few precious hints for fishermen who have already acquired the rudiments of the piscatorial art."—*Glasgow Herald*.

"We commend the little book as a very good and inexpensive practical guide."—*Aberdeen Free Press*.

"It may safely be pronounced as the most practical and instructive work of its kind, and at its price, in the literature of angling."—*Dundee Advertiser*.

"Full of valuable hints and suggestions, conveyed in a fashion which most happily combines conciseness and clearness."—*Scottish Leader*.

"The book will be found eminently useful, not only by experienced anglers, but in the case of beginners it will prove a most invaluable companion and adviser."—*Oban Times*.

HOW TO CATCH TROUT

BY

THREE ANGLERS

FOURTH EDITION

EDINBURGH: DAVID DOUGLAS
1889

[*All rights reserved*]

PREFACE.

This volume contains a series of essays, by different writers, on the art of trout-fishing. The aim of the authors has been to compress, within the narrowest possible limits, such practical information and advice as will enable a beginner, without further instruction, to attain moderate proficiency in the use of every legitimate lure. In carrying out this design their endeavour has been to avoid unnecessary technicality, to steer clear of "fads," and to confine themselves to statements likely to receive the general assent of experienced anglers.

To make the work as complete as possible a chapter has been added containing a brief statement of the Law of Scotland relating to trout-fishing. This, which is believed to be a novelty in angling literature, may be of service to readers who are not versed in legal lore.

Although the authors are most familiar with the streams and lochs of Scotland, they are not without the hope that what they have to say may also be found useful by their brethren south of the Tweed.

EDINBURGH, *April* 1888.

CONTENTS.

CHAP.		PAGE
I.	Wet or Sunk Fly-fishing,	1
II.	Dry Fly-fishing,	25
III.	Worm-fishing,	29
IV.	Minnow-fishing,	46
V.	Creeper and May-fly Fishing,	56
VI.	Loch-fishing,	61
VII.	Some Hints as to Tackle,	70
VIII.	The Law of Scotland as to Trout-fishing,	76

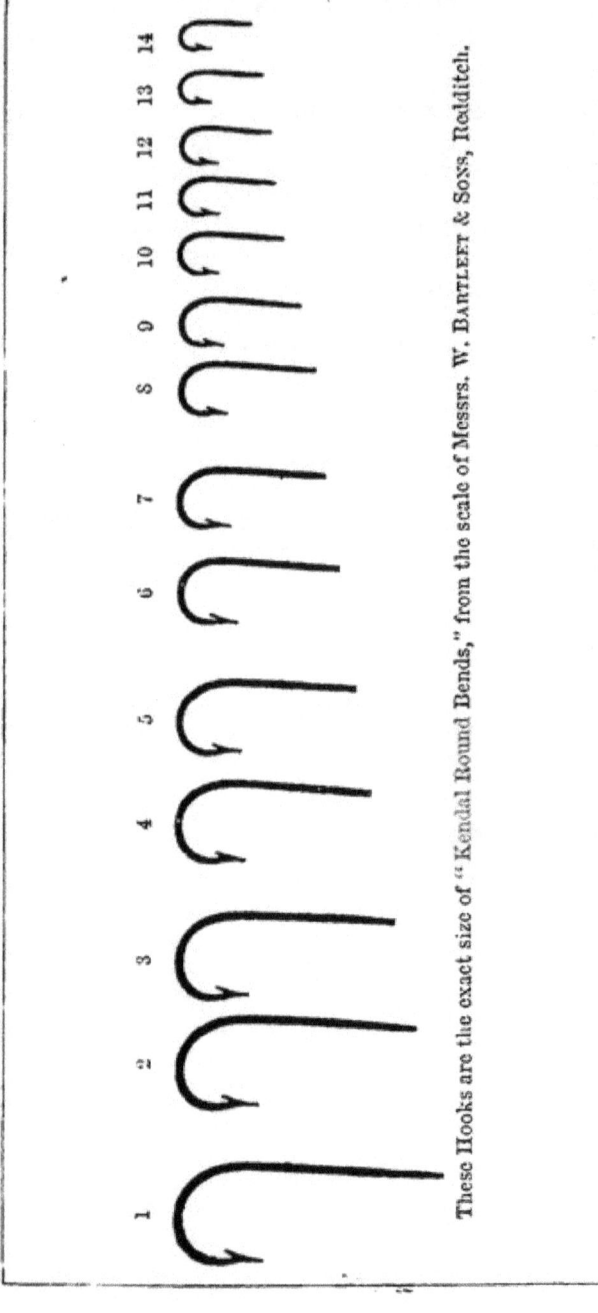

These Hooks are the exact size of "Kendal Round Bends," from the scale of Messrs. W. BARTLEET & SONS, Redditch.

CHAPTER I.

WET OR SUNK FLY-FISHING.

This style of angling is almost universally adopted in Scotland, and is also common in many parts of England. Although it may not call for such minute study of insect life as is considered necessary by the votaries of dry fly-fishing, it demands an even greater knowledge of the habits and haunts of trout; while in point of excitement and variety it falls in no way short of the rival method.

Rod.—For wet fly-fishing we prefer a light one-handed rod of moderate stiffness, measuring from 9 to 12 feet in length. For a few of the broadest rivers, however, where it is sometimes necessary to cast a very long line, a two-handed rod, 13 or 14 feet in length, may be found more serviceable.

Opinions differ so much as to the best material for rod-making that we think it advisable to leave this matter entirely to the taste of the angler. There is one point, however, as to which it is impossible to be too emphatic,—and that is, in warning the beginner against the use of a rod in the least degree too heavy. The neglect of this caution is bound to lead to slovenly and therefore unsuccessful fishing. The moment the arm gets tired the casting becomes clumsy, the interest flags, and if a trout be induced to rise he is either noticed too late or struck in such a listless fashion that he escapes without difficulty.

REEL.—In selecting a reel it is necessary to see that it is of the proper weight to balance the rod, and runs easily. A ratchet of moderate strength is of great assistance in running a heavy trout, but if too strong it is a constant source of danger.

LINE.—The line may be of hair, silk and hair, undressed silk, or waterproofed silk; all of these are good. Its weight and thickness should bear some proportion to the size and stiffness of the rod; and except in the case of the very finest lines, one or two yards of tapered twisted gut should be spliced to the end. Experience will show that this is an important aid to casting.

GUT.—The gut casting-line, for a beginner, should not be more than nine feet long. The first two or three strands should be rather thicker than the others, and should taper gradually down from the end of the twisted gut. The remainder should be of the best quality that can be obtained, special care being taken to ensure that its different lengths are perfectly round and free from blemishes. As to the thickness, the angler must be guided by circumstances. A beginner, however, will find it much easier to cast with stoutish gut, and if it be of good quality, and be dropped lightly on the water, he will have more success with it than with finer gut badly handled. We believe thoroughly, however, in the efficacy of fine gut on all waters which are much fished, and strongly advise every angler to accustom himself to its use. It must not be understood, however, that we consider drawn gut necessary, or even advantageous, under all circumstances. Early in the season before the waters have shrunk to their summer level; later in the year when the rivers are running full after a flood; or, even when they are low and clear, if a strong wind be blowing, good undrawn gut will be found quite as deadly. By using it, moreover, time will be saved in landing the trout, and no fisher need be told how this will affect his take at the end of the day.

FLIES.—We now come to the most important element in the matter of tackle—to wit, the flies themselves; and here it is necessary to explain that in our Lowland streams two distinct types of artificial flies are used—the winged fly and the spider or hackle. Of these, the winged fly is undoubtedly the closer imitation of the natural insect as we see it playing on the surface of the water. One would think that, in competition with it, the spider, which is nothing more than a few fibres of feather twisted round the shank of the hook, must be left hopelessly in the rear. This is not, however, the experience of many of the most skilful and successful anglers in the north of England as well as in the south of Scotland. Indeed, for *fishing up stream,* in comparatively rapid waters, we have no hesitation in saying that the hackle is the more deadly of the two.

It is of supreme importance that the flies—whether winged or hackled—should be dressed on the finest gut, and should not be too bulky. At the best, the finest feather is clumsy and coarse compared with the delicate gossamer of the insect wing, and naturally the more of the former there is, the more likely is the trout to detect the deception. The wings should be divided or "split," as it is technically called, and should, in the great majority of flies, be dressed so as to stand well out from the shank of the hook. For the body we do not care as a rule for anything more than either a strip of quill—which makes one of the best imitations of the natural insect—or, even simpler, the coloured thread with which the hook is tied to the gut. Early in the season, however, a heavier body is often found advantageous, and this, if desired, can be made of "hare lug," water-rat or mole fur, floss silk, or mohair wool. But in no case should more be used than is sufficient to cover the shank of the hook. For a large or coloured water a little tinsel may be added, but when the rivers are small and clear this is unnecessary.

As a general rule it is advisable, in all rivers which are much fished, to use an artificial fly considerably smaller than the insect it is intended to represent. When a strong wind is blowing, however, or the river is running full, a size more nearly approaching nature may be used.

In wet or sunk fly-fishing the number of hooks used by experts varies from two to eight, or even ten, but three or four may be put down as the average. For a beginner our advice is to use no more than two, or, at most, three, as he will find that the hooks have an objectionable tendency to catch not only each other, but also the clothes, basket, and other belongings of the angler. Even for one who has acquired some skill in casting, we do not think there is much to be gained by using more than four. The only important advantage that we can see in a larger number is that it offers the trout a variety of choice, and so increases the probability of the particular fly they are feeding on—if, as too often happens, they are capricious—being discovered. But this seems more than counterbalanced by the difficulty in managing the extra hooks.

As instructions for making up a casting-line,

with descriptions of different knots, are given in the chapter on tackle, it is only necessary to give here a few hints on the subject. The bob-flies, or droppers, as they are termed, should be attached at intervals varying, according to the size and number used, from two to three feet. In no case must a loop be employed for fastening any of the hooks—it is clumsy in the extreme, and is apt to cause an unnatural break or ripple on the surface of the water. The length of the droppers should not exceed two to three inches. If longer, the gut gets twisted round the casting-line, and the fly is rendered practically useless.

We shall now give a list of flies that we have found to be good killers throughout the season. It has, of course, no pretension to being exhaustive, but we believe there are few days, from April to September, on which one or other of them will not meet the fancy of the trout.

March Brown, male and female. A good fly for a mild day in April.

Blue Dun and Iron Blue Dun. Most reliable flies during April and May, especially in cold weather.

Greenwell's Glory. A standard spring fly.

Woodcock Wing, with (*a*) hare-lug body; (*b*) quill body, and red or black hackle; (*c*) yellow or orange silk body and red hackle; (*d*) black silk body and black hackle. In one or other of these shapes this is, in our experience, the most reliable of all the winged flies.

Grouse Wing, with yellow or orange silk body, and red hackle. A favourite in some of the larger rivers in spring and autumn.

Grouse Spider, with dark red or orange body. Sometimes kills well in spring and autumn.

Partridge Spider. Made from the ruddy-brown hackle feather of the partridge. Body, orange, yellow, dark red, or purple silk. We almost never fish without this fly, and find that throughout the whole season it is a certain killer.

Grey Partridge Spider. Sometimes good in spring and towards dusk on a summer evening.

Sand Fly. Appears in some rivers early in May, and is fed upon greedily.

Dotterel Spider, with yellow silk body, and

Cinnamon Fly. Do well in some rivers during late spring and early summer.

Yellow Dun. A capital fly, from middle of May to middle of June.

Golden Plover Spider, with quill or dark orange body. Good in early summer.

Red Quill Gnat. Also good in early summer.

Black Spider, with quill, orange silk, or dark red silk body; and spider made of black starling feather, with white tip. Both these flies are good all through the summer, when rivers are low and clear.

Autumn Red or *Dun*. Often very deadly in September.

Red Spider, with yellow silk body. Best in a slightly-coloured water.

Teal Wing, with (*a*) orange silk body and red hackle (this is known as the Professor); (*b*) black silk body and black hackle. Should be used in a large water when coloured.

In addition to these flies, the angler should have a collection of dun-coloured spiders, of different shades, made from the small, soft feathers of such birds as the starling, blackbird, snipe, water-hen, or sea-swallow. One or other of these will afford a sufficiently exact imitation of any dun for which the trout may show a decided partiality.

CASTING.—The first, and in many respects the most important matter to be learned in fly-fishing is, how to throw out or "cast" the line. It is difficult to give directions for accomplishing this apparently simple operation which will suit all circumstances, but the following general hints may be found useful :—

Begin with a short line—one of not more than 15 feet in length will suffice. Considerable force should be used in drawing it from the water so as to ensure that it is fully extended behind the angler before the forward motion is begun; and this backward motion should also have an upward

WET OR SUNK FLY-FISHING. 9

tendency, in order that the hooks may be kept clear of the banks behind. The forward motion should be begun *the very instant*—but not before—the line is fully extended. The force necessary in this part of the cast depends entirely on circumstances. With a stiff rod, or a long line, or against a strong wind, considerable exertion may be required; otherwise, the spring of the rod, with but a slight motion of the wrist, will suffice to carry out the flies. As a rule, the forward impetus should be stopped when the point of the rod is well up in the air, the rod being simply allowed to follow the line, or even to check its motion, until the flies touch the water. Should it be necessary, however, to cast against the wind, or if a high bank or trees behind prevent the line being extended backwards, it will be found better to bring down the point of the rod sharply to within a yard or so of the water, and then stop its motion abruptly. To prevent the line doubling up, the rod should be brought round the angler's head in a circular direction. The cast should be made as much as possible from the wrist, the arm from the shoulder to the elbow being kept close in to the side: this not only saves labour, but adds to the grace and efficiency of the throw. Finally, it should be kept in view that the rod is intended to aid in the work, and its spring should therefore be utilised so as to reduce muscular exertion to a minimum.

UP AND DOWN STREAM FISHING.—As has been already indicated, there are two modes of fishing,—up-stream and down-stream,—and it is now necessary to say something as to their respective merits. In the former the angler works his way *up* the river, casting his line above him, and never allowing it to float past him; in the latter the line is cast across or down stream and allowed to float downwards. It can hardly be doubted that up-stream fishing is theoretically the better style to adopt. Its advantages, as set forth by Mr. Stewart in the *Practical Angler*, have never been successfully controverted. As the trout lie with their heads facing the current, it stands to reason that they are less likely to be alarmed if approached from the rear; a shorter line can thus be used, it is much easier to strike gently with the current than against it, and in running a trout it is only the water already fished over that is disturbed. These are all most important considerations, but, as usual, there are two sides to the question. In fishing up stream, the flies are carried more quickly downwards, and they are apt, especially in a current of any depth, unless when the trout are on the surface looking out for the natural insect, to be swept past unnoticed. Moreover, wading up a large river, or even one of moderate size, if slightly flooded, entails very much greater labour; and the direction of the wind often makes up-stream fishing impossible. Having thus given briefly some of the *pros* and *cons* on this vexed question, we shall at present content ourselves with saying that in our opinion the best plan is to adopt a judicious combination of the two methods of fishing.

STRIKING.—When a rise is seen or felt the trout ought in up-stream fishing to be struck at once. This is done by a simple motion of the wrist, which must be both instantaneous and gentle. No habit is more easily acquired, and more dangerous, than that of violent striking, and every angler should endeavour to keep his nerves well under control, and so learn to avoid the startled jerk which so often leads to the loss of a sonsy trout. In down-stream fishing the weight of the fish itself, aided by the current, is sufficient to drive the hook home, and all that is required is a slight tightening of the line. In many cases, however, even this will be found unnecessary. A heavy trout will often take the fly without breaking the surface, and be firmly hooked at the same moment its presence is felt by the angler.

We think that as a general rule it is better to keep a finger on the line while fishing. When this is done, a gentle pull at the fly is more quickly felt, and the effect of the strike is more instantaneous. It is necessary, of course, to raise the finger as soon as the trout is hooked; but after a little practice it will be found that this is done instinctively. Striking from the reel may be required when only large trout are to be looked for, but in most of our Scotch rivers the plan we recommend is perfectly safe.

LANDING TROUT.—After the trout is hooked, it ought, if a small one, to be basketed in the quietest and most expeditious manner possible. One of any size, however, cannot be dealt with in this summary fashion; indeed the process of running a heavy trout with a small hook and fine tackle requires the utmost skill and caution. The moment it is fast the line should be allowed to run freely from the reel, and the point of the rod raised to the perpendicular. At first no more strain should be brought to bear than is necessary to keep the line tight, but as the trout becomes exhausted he can be kept more in check. The exact amount of pressure to be exercised can only be learned by experience, but it is better to err on the side of gentleness. A slack line, however, is to be avoided above all things, as it will almost certainly enable the trout either to expel the hook from his mouth or to break the tackle by a sudden rush. If he should leap into the air the point of the rod must be lowered at once, only, however, to be raised again the instant he regains his native element. The angler should always endeavour to keep further down stream than his prey, otherwise he will have to contend against the weight of the trout *plus* that of the current.

If a landing-net is carried—and in rivers of any size it will be found a great convenience—it should be used in water not less than a foot deep: a trout, when stranded on a shallow, struggles in a most dangerous fashion. The net should further be kept well below the surface, so as to avoid startling the fish, and to keep the meshes clear of the flies. When no net is carried the trout should be led gently into the side, at a point, if possible, where the shore shelves gradually down to the water, and his snout brought closely up to the channel or bank. This done, he must next be lifted with the hand out of the water, the line being on no account touched until he is safe on the shore.

CONCEALMENT.—The main secret of success in all fishing undoubtedly lies in keeping out of sight of the trout. Casting up stream, as we have seen, aids greatly in this ; but it is also necessary to take care that the angler's shadow is not allowed to fall on the water he is to fish ; to keep off high banks as much as possible ; and to utilise any natural shelter such as that afforded by bushes or trees. It is also possible to keep out of sight by throwing a long line; but this should only be resorted to when all other resources fail.

MANAGEMENT OF LINE.—It is further of great importance that the flies should be allowed to float naturally down with the current. Any motion of the rod or dragging of the line, which causes a disturbance on the surface of the water, should be carefully avoided. As a rule, it is better to allow the flies, especially if spiders are used, to sink a little, as when this is done the trout seem less able to detect the deception. When they are rising freely to the natural insect, however, it is often profitable to keep the flies on the surface. This can be accomplished by casting frequently, and by raising the point of the rod as the line floats towards the angler.

In fly-fishing it will be found that a large proportion of the trout which rise escape—some without even touching the hooks, others after nothing more than a gentle pull. This is to some extent unavoidable, but the number of captures may be increased by using the shortest line consistent with the necessary concealment, by quick striking, and by keeping the line as straight as possible from the point of the rod to the flies. If the angler be striking from the reel, he may, if the trout are not hooking well, try the experiment of keeping his finger on the line, and we shall be surprised if the result do not convert him to our way of thinking. Great care should be taken, especially when fishing still water on the further side of a strong current, to allow as little of the line above the flies to touch the water as possible. When this is not attended to, the middle of the line curves, and before the effect of the "strike" reaches the hook the trout has gone on its way rejoicing.

How to Fish a Small Stream.—A river which can be cast over without wading should under almost all circumstances be fished up stream. The lower portion of each pool, which is nearly always smooth and comparatively still, with a glass-like surface, need only be fished when there is enough breeze to cause a ripple. When there is a strong wind blowing, however, the shallow water just above where the stream breaks should always be tried, as feeding-trout often congregate there. But in a bright, still day, the first cast should be made about the point where the rough water of the stream comes to an end. The line should be thrown up and across so that the tail-fly shall just reach the opposite bank; the flies, with as little of the rest of the line touching the water as possible, should be allowed to float down with the stream until they are almost opposite the fisher, when they should be lifted and the same process repeated—the next cast, however, being made a little further up and more into the middle of the stream. This done, yet another cast should be made almost straight up, the flies being simply allowed to light on the edge of the current next the angler. It is useless in this cast to keep the line in the water for any time, as the stream at once forces the gut back in coils. If a trout rises, but does not touch the hook, another throw should be made a short distance above where it broke the water; and every trout seen rising "to itself" should be cast over in the same way.

When a strong wind blowing down stream makes fishing up impossible, the best plan is to keep well back from the water's edge, and cast as nearly straight across as circumstances permit. The line should never, unless when no other course is practicable, be cast down stream, and should only be allowed to travel a few yards.

Rivers of this kind, which are generally rapid running and shallow, and contain great numbers of small fish, should be fished as rapidly as possible. Except when a trout has risen but missed the fly, a cast in any particular spot should seldom be repeated, and the angler should walk as quickly as possible from one stream to another. Where the basket has to be made up of small trout, quick fishing is absolutely necessary.

How to Fish a River of Medium Size.—Streams of a larger size, such as can only be cast over with the aid of wading, ought to be fished in much the same way as those we have been describing. In them, however, up-stream casting is not so essential, and more consideration may be given to the direction of the wind. With a favourable, or even a contrary breeze, if light, a good plan is to fish up the shallow side of the stream, and then, wading well in, to fish down the further side, casting close in to the edge. Special attention ought to be given to all places where there is a high bank, or bushes on the opposite side, as the trout in such spots, not being disturbed by passers-by, are both more numerous and not so shy as in more exposed stretches of water.

How to Fish a Large River.—Large rivers which cannot be fully commanded even with the aid of wading, are generally best fished down and across; but the edges of the streams on the nearer side may often be worked to advantage upwards. This will depend on the depth and strength of the current; but as a rule there is sufficient volume of water in a large river to conceal even the down-stream fisher, provided he throws a moderately long line. Rivers of this kind, and of the class last considered, should be fished slowly. When the trout are found rising at a particular place it is well to remain there as long as the take lasts: by moving from one spot to another valuable time may be lost.

SEASON OF THE YEAR.

April.—The fly-fishing season begins at a date varying, with the weather and the country through which the streams flow, from the beginning to the end of April. During this month the trout, in almost every river of any size, are gradually getting into condition. Each mild day quantities of March browns and other flies are hatched and greedily fed upon; and during the latter half of April, when the weather is favourable, large baskets are often caught. Early in the month the trout lie for the most part in the deepish and comparatively gentle currents, and only come to the surface when the flies are floating down in considerable numbers. In the afternoon, however, they generally haunt the shallow water at the foot of pools, where they seem to feed on larvæ or imperfectly hatched insects. At this time—generally from three to five o'clock—they can often, especially after a cold day, be captured, if the surface of the stream be rippled, by allowing the flies to sink more than usual. The time of the take, however, when the largest and best trout are to be looked for, is earlier, at a time varying with the appearance of the flies, from eleven to two o'clock. When the trout are seen rising in numbers there is most prospect of success by casting up stream and keeping the flies near the surface of the water; but otherwise we think it better, at this time of the year, to throw straight across and allow the flies to float slowly down for a few yards. As a rule we find that in spring and autumn we meet with most success when the flies are well sunk.

In spring the pools and streams best sheltered from the prevailing wind, and those to which the sun's rays penetrate freely, afford the best sport. Whenever a strong wind is blowing, a sheltered spot should be sought for. Although a gentle breeze is rather an advantage than otherwise, a gale drives the flies off the water, and trout are rarely on the lookout for this kind of food unless the natural insect is seen in large numbers. The best flies for April are the March brown, blue-dun, woodcock wing with hare-lug body and tinsel, and Greenwell's glory. In bright weather, with low water, a partridge spider may be substituted for the March brown, and the woodcock wing used without the hare-lug. The size of hook should vary from Nos. 9 to 11.[1]

May.—In the month of May fly-fishing is general throughout the whole country. The

---

[1] The numbers mentioned here are those of Messrs. W. Bartleet & Son's "Kendal Round-Bends." Should hooks of another maker or pattern be preferred, the corresponding number can easily be ascertained.

trout, gradually increasing in strength, spread themselves over the strong currents and shallow water. They have sufficient vitality to withstand the effects of a cold night; the supply of flies is not so precarious as during the previous month; and sport is altogether more reliable. The take generally lasts during the greater part of the day, commencing about nine o'clock and continuing till about five or six o'clock, with a break, however, of two or three hours some time after midday. The trout being now found in shallower water, up-stream fishing is most essential, and quick casting is necessary. The best flies are partridge spider, woodcock wing (without hare-lug), and lighter duns than those recommended for April. Towards the middle or end of May the yellow dun may be used with great effect. The hooks should run from Nos. 11 to 14.

June.—With the advent of June fly-fishing in the early rivers becomes uncertain. When the May or stone-fly is on the water good sport may often be had with small artificial fly; but, as a rule, if reliable fishing of this kind is wished, it is better to take to the smaller and later streams. There large baskets may still be had with hooks of the same kind and size as recommended for May. On the larger waters a great change takes place when the May-fly disappears—usually about the middle of the month. Except after a flood, and often not even then, a general rise is rarely seen. Flies are hovering over the water in thousands, but the trout let them pass unheeded. Some sport, however, may still be had by casting over stray rising fish, using the very finest gut and smallest midge flies, or recourse may be had to dry fly-fishing. When the trout are feeding freely, the flies mentioned as best for May, with the addition of the black spider, but a size smaller, should be used. Late in the month it will be found more profitable to fish with nothing but a selection of the very smallest dun spiders, of the shades most nearly approaching those of the insects upon which the trout are seen to be feeding.

July.—During the day-time in July the trout feed for the most part on worms and minnows, and it is only by casting delicately over rising fish that any sport can be obtained with artificial fly.

EVENING FISHING.—But nearly always towards sunset, and frequently all through the darkness, especially in warm weather, the trout rise freely. So long as the twilight lingers small flies should be used; indeed the tiniest midge will often prove most successful. After darkness has set in the rise generally ceases for a short time, which the angler may employ in putting on larger flies. In our experience it does not matter much what pattern is used, but we have found a small loch size very successful. A most useful fly for such fishing is dressed thus: wings, white or brown owl feather; legs, a few fibres of same; body, thick floss silk[1]; tag of wash leather. At night a cast of two flies only should be used, as otherwise it is difficult to avoid ravelling. Drawn gut is quite unnecessary, and as the angler is concealed by the darkness, he need not throw a long line or fish up stream. The best places are the shallows at the foot of large pools, but sport is often to be got in the deep, still water. The streams, however, are utterly useless, and should be passed over. The heaviest trout often come close in to the banks to feed, and the sides of the pool should therefore be cast over carefully. The best mode of fishing is to throw repeatedly in different directions, allowing the flies to rest on the surface for a moment, and then drawing them slowly and steadily across the current. Every foot of likely water should be fished over slowly, and all rises to the natural fly, no matter how insignificant they may seem, should receive attention. As the slightest unnatural ripple is sufficient to disturb the trout in the still, shallow water, where they are generally found, there must be as little splashing as possible when wading.

August.—The greater part of August may be set down as a blank so far as river fly-fishing is concerned. Sport in the evening is rendered un-

[1] Yellow or white.

certain by the chill autumnal air which is frequently experienced after sunset; and during the day the trout resolutely refuse to look at the most skilfully thrown imitation of the natural insect.

BURN FISHING.—But a heavy basket—it is better, however, not to speak of the average—can be got by making for the nearest hill burn which has pools large enough to permit of a fly being thrown over them. This kind of fishing has its own charms, and may serve to tide over an otherwise barren time. For a burn not more than one, or at most two, flies ought to be used, and all that the angler has to do is to keep out of sight and get his line on the water somehow. If he does not make too much splash he may be tolerably certain of a rise in each pool, and he will probably be startled at the amount of resistance offered by some little fellow not weighing more than two or three ounces.

September.—Towards the end of August, and all through September, good sport is frequently had with fly, especially if, as is often the case at this time of the year, the rivers are running full after a flood. Early in September the trout are still to be found in the stronger streams, but as the month glides on they gradually fall back to the quieter water. The most of what has been said as to the mode of fishing and flies to be used in April applies to this season; but as the trout have had the benefit of half a year's experience of the wiles of men, smaller hooks and finer tackle are required. The only additional fly that need be mentioned is the autumn red or dun, which frequently appears in great numbers throughout September.

CHAPTER II.

DRY FLY-FISHING.

As the season advances and trout become warier, the method of dry fly-fishing, so much in vogue in England, may often be useful.

We suspect that a prime reason why this method is so little used here in the North, is not so much conservatism nor laziness, nor even the unsuitability of our waters, as an idea that special tackle and flies must be got for its practice—an idea quite fallacious. Ordinary flies tied on gut are at least as good for the purpose as those dressed upon eyed hooks, so far as our experience goes, except that greater care has to be taken during the drying process, lest the gut at the neck of the hook become cracked and the fly whip off, or even worse, break in the mouth of—of course a big one.

What is requisite in flies for dry fly-fishing is as accurate an imitation of the fly on which trout are feeding as can be made, accurate imitation being an essential in this case; and yet this need not be made a hard and fast rule, as a properly dressed spider will usually kill at least as well as any winged fly, the former being made with plenty of hackle to make it float.

In other respects the tackle is the same as that used for wet fly-fishing, the only difference being that no more than one fly is attached when using it dry.

The method here employed is generally upstream casting, done thus :— A good fish having been observed rising, angler approaches the bank cautiously, and a good deal below his victim, then after carefully measuring with his eye the distance, lets out the exact quantity of line required, and before casting dries the single fly with which his line is armed, by either causing it to describe three or four slow figures of eight overhead, or a like number of circles, then with an underhand or horizontal cast, which is best adapted for this style of fishing, he aims at a point some six inches or a foot above the fish. Now comes the most difficult and most essential part of the whole process. The line ought to be cast so as to allow of its being somewhat slack just at the time of the fly touching the surface; so that it may cock properly, *i.e.* sit on the water naturally, right end up, and next may float over the fish without any drag from the line. If the fish rise, he is to be hooked by a gentle twitch of the wrist, hardly to be called a strike; if not, the fly is to be allowed to float well down before lifting it for another cast, lest the fish be scared.

A repetition of this process of drying the fly, and casting over fish which are seen rising, constitutes the somewhat monotonous but certainly artistic method of dry fly-fishing, which, however, does not call for so intimate a knowledge of fish nature as the method of fly-fishing ordinarily pursued here.

A judicious combination of these two styles may be recommended, the dry fly being used on still waters and pools, with or without a ripple, and on slow streams; whilst the wet is employed to search the more rapid waters.

The angler in this way may attain more success than by a rigid adherence to either method.

We do not attempt to give a list of flies, only a few of our favourites, close imitation of the natural insect being the main point to be aimed at.

1. *March Brown.* In spring.
2. *Hare Lug* and *Woodcock*, quill body. All the season.
3. *Hare Lug* and *Blae Wing*, quill body. All the season.
4. *Hare Lug* and *Yellowish Blae Wing*, quill body. In autumn.
5. *Grey Quill Gnat.* All the season.

6. *Red Quill Gnat.* From May onwards.
7. *Black Spider*, quill body or brown silk body. From May onwards.
8. *Starling Tipped Spider*, quill body. From May onwards.
9. *Corncrake Spider*, quill body. From May onwards.
10. *Dotterel* or *Snipe Spider*, quill body. From May onwards.
11. *Small Blae Wing*, with dark watermouse legs, black silk body. May and June.
12. *Olive Gnat.* April and May.

CHAPTER III.

WORM-FISHING.

WORM-FISHING in small clear waters is popular with most anglers. Although less artistic than fly-fishing, it requires an equal dexterity, and even greater knowledge of the haunts and habits of trout.

During the summer months the worm is a very deadly bait; indeed, the accomplished angler can rely on it for sport with greater certainty than with any other lure. The beginner will soon attain considerable proficiency if he make it a rule always to fish up stream, and be careful to observe the character of the water in which trout are lying.

In the first place, we offer a few remarks about equipment.

ROD.—The rod should be 14 or 15 feet in length, and at the same time light and stiff. The one we like best consists of hollow cane for the butt and centre, with a top piece made of hickory and lance-wood. Besides being easy to cast with, a rod of this description commands, with a moderate length of line, every variety of water. Although apparently a small matter to write about, we here caution our readers against having their rods highly varnished. At no period of the angling season is this of greater importance than at midsummer, as the trout then lie in the shallowest water, and easily perceive the angler's approach. To dull the rod a simple process commends itself, viz. to rub it with wet earth or clay. This dries in a minute, and completely covers any glitter.

Reel.—A reel in proportion to the rod not only looks better, but improves the balance considerably.

Line.—Silk and hair make a capital line, which lasts a long time.

Casting-Line.—The gut cast should not be shorter than two, nor exceed three yards in length. The lower portion should consist of drawn gut, and above it the best undrawn, tapering towards the reel line, while the addition of a few feet triple gut or twisted horse hair, will be found of service in casting. Much, however, depends on the character of the weather. The angler will at times require to shorten his gut cast to suit the wind, while on calm days the addition of a few strands of finest gut is necessary.

TACKLE.—The tackle, composed of either two or three small hooks, is now almost universally used. Some anglers, however, still hold by the single hook. For small clear streams we much prefer the former, but find that the latter does best in spated waters. If the worms are small enough, a tackle composed of two hooks should be used, but three hooks if the worms exceed 2½ inches in length. Numbers 10, 11, and 12,[1] round- or sneck-bend, are good sizes for the tackle, and No. 4 or 5 round-bend for the single hook—a size or two larger being used during a flood. It is a great mistake to have very small hooks on the tackle; the angler may get more bites, but he will certainly not hook so well as with a larger size.

BAITING.—When baiting, the worm is held between the thumb and forefinger of left hand. The lowest hook of the tackle is then inserted a moderate distance from the head, the centre hook about the middle, and the uppermost near the tail. The barbs should be freely exposed; this prevents the bait from coming off, and hooks with greater certainty. Care is also necessary to have the worm equally distributed over the tackle, so that too much of it is not allowed to hang at either end.

From this description it will be seen that the

[1] These numbers are from Bartleet's scale for Kendal round- and sneck-bend hooks.

head is placed lowest: this is not of much importance; when reversed the worm is equally attractive. To bait the single hook the barb is entered close to the head and worked down the centre of the worm, without breaking the skin, to within half an inch of the tail. The bait requires to be frequently examined; if broken or dead a fresh worm should at once be substituted.

To carry worms we always employ a tin box, attached round the waist by means of a broad leather strap. It will be found more secure and more convenient for baiting than a bag.

WORMS.—For a day's fishing a gross to a gross and a half of worms is necessary. These should be carried in the basket in a large flannel bag containing plenty of moss, a supply from time to time being transferred to the tin box as required. In this way worms may be kept fresh all day. Some attention is required to have them in good condition; they ought to be scoured in clean moss for a few days, and care taken that it does not become too dry. We occasionally sprinkle a small quantity of cream over them. In this way the fine pink colour is soon acquired, pleasing both to the eyes of angler and trout. If it is unwise to make use of fresh gathered worms, there is a danger of running into the opposite extreme by keeping them until they lose much of their vitality.

We think it unnecessary in this short paper to describe the various kinds of worms; we simply advise the angler to use them as small as possible, except during a spate.

CASTING.—In casting, the line is carried back with an easy swing and urged forward with more or less force according to circumstances, the rod top making more of a circle than in fly-fishing. If a long line is being used, or if the wind is blowing down stream, the point of the rod must be lowered almost to the surface of the water. This causes the worm to fall lightly and the line to be fully extended. The rod is then slowly raised, leaving only a few feet of gut in the stream. It is difficult to perform this last movement, great delicacy of touch being required, for if done too quickly the worm is dragged down stream. A short line does not require the rod to be lowered to the same extent, and is more easily managed.

On other occasions the rod top requires to be kept well raised. Take, for example, a cast over a rough current to quieter water beyond. If the line is all immersed, the strong rush at once pulls the worm from the desired spot; whereas, if only a few feet of gut are permitted to alight, the intervening current has no power over it. This is best accomplished by checking the forward movement of the rod, and not lowering the point as we have already alluded to.

The angler, it will thus be seen, has often to vary his style of casting to suit different kinds of water, and in like manner the length of his line; but 10 to 15 feet on ordinary-sized streams is long enough to fish most places.

THE STRIKE.—The strike is easily accomplished; it consists in tightening the line down stream. Anglers are usually far too rough. The small wires forming the tackle are exceedingly sharp, and take firm hold with a minimum of force. This pull or strike when using the tackle must be instantaneous with the first indications of a bite, but should never be a sudden jerk. This is sometimes done involuntarily, and should be guarded against, as it is certain to result in breakages. If only a small quantity of line is kept in the water, there should be no difficulty in the matter. The bite is then easily perceived, and the point of the rod being always in advance of the worm, it is only natural to pull down stream. Beginners should remember to place uppermost the hand nearest the river; this of itself is sufficient to ensure the correct direction of the strike, but it lies entirely with the angler to estimate the requisite amount of force. We have said that every bite should be responded to at once. Now if too much line is kept in the stream, the angler has no exact knowledge where his bait really is; a trout may have taken and expelled it, or have swallowed it, without any perceptible stoppage of the line. Of course in the latter case the fish cannot escape, but if the take is on, much valuable time is wasted in cutting out the hooks. We therefore once more impress on our readers the advantages of keeping little line in the water. Although often overlooked, it is one of the most important rules to remember, and it makes all the difference between an average and a first-class worm-fisher.

TIME OF YEAR.—Trout take the worm throughout the whole fishing season, but it is only during June and July that it forms their principal food. We only advocate its use after the May fly-fishing is over, when trout, glutted with insect food, betake themselves to bottom feeding. Splendid sport may then be enjoyed, which can be depended on if the rivers are small and clear, and the weather settled.

Before worm-fishing properly commences good takes may sometimes be made during May in the early morning, if mild. Trout are then feeding on the creeper, and will occasionally take a worm quite as readily. The angler, however, should be provided with both lures.

When June has run for a week or two, worm-fishing may be pursued at such quarters as St. Boswell's on the Tweed, and Chirnside on the lower Whitadder. At both these places the fishing is early, and lasts for a shorter period than in smaller streams. Daybreak is the best time for catching big trout, and the forenoon can generally be relied on; but fish in large rivers are very capricious, a slight change in the weather not unfrequently putting them off the feed entirely. In small waters such as Leader and Gala, the take is more certain, and continues a longer time. These streams are admirably adapted for worm-fishing, and sport can be depended on from the middle of June to nearly the end of July. During June, in rivers of this size, trout feed at nearly every hour of the day. We mention three distinct takes. The first commences in the early morning, say at two or three o'clock, if the weather is at all favourable; the next about eight, which extends more or less up to one or two P.M.; and lastly an afternoon take, between four and six o'clock. It will be observed that as the day advances trout leave the broken water and lie at the tail ends of pools and streams. A good breeze is then of great importance.

At the beginning of July there is occasionally a touch of frost or fog, which spoils the early morning take; when it is warm, however, trout still feed freely during the early hours. The best time of day is now from eight to two or three o'clock, and it is curious to note that the afternoon take is gradually discontinued after the first week of July.

Our readers must not suppose that these hours are kept very precisely. If the weather is settled, there is little variation from day to day, but frost, want of sunshine, and many other causes, may retard the take for hours. Neither is it to be imagined that trout do not feed except at the hours mentioned; fairly good sport may be got in smaller streams all through the day, but nothing to be compared to what is enjoyed when the feeding is general.

As July draws to an end, trout show no special relish for worms unless under very favourable conditions. For two or three weeks at this season, or up to the middle of August, they take fly and worm very badly. May this be owing to their feeding on the Caddis or immature autumn flies? Our experience favours this theory. At any rate, when these flies appear towards the end of the month, it is certain that trout take them greedily, and continue doing so during September.

WHERE TO FISH.—In June and July trout scatter themselves over the shallows; in fact they may be captured in water hardly deep enough to cover them. This is important to keep in mind. It points out the character of water in which the best sport is to be obtained

The expert fills his basket in places that are usually passed over earlier in the season. That many anglers do so even during the worm months is clearly shown by their poor takes. They somehow prefer the deep strong rushes, of all places the least reliable. The beginner should miss over no water, however unproductive it may appear to his eyes.

WEATHER.—Nothing helps the worm-fisher more than sunshine; favoured with this, a moderate breeze, and occasional showers, his sport is almost a certainty. A close day with drizzling rain is good, and also one with a cloudless sky. Trout may be caught in all weathers; even on what may be termed an unfavourable day, viz. one with dark clouds and a boisterous wind, the angler may be successful by adopting the method explained hereafter for fishing still water.

A good breeze is of great importance; it opens up stretches of water at other times practically unfishable. Of course when it is very strong it is troublesome for casting; yet on the whole we much prefer moderate wind to calm weather; it gives the angler a variety of fishing. On still days he is confined to the streams, but wind brings into capital order many portions of the river that afford quite as good sport as the broken water.

We shall now endeavour to describe how best to fish a river, and for the sake of clearness, make our remarks under the two following divisions:—

1*st*. Broken water of every kind not dependent on wind.

2*d*. Still water for the most part only fishable when there is wind.

HOW TO FISH BROKEN WATER, STREAMS, etc.—To fish these to best advantage considerable skill and method are required. It is easy enough for any one to take a trout from a good run, but it is quite another thing to basket half a dozen.

The angler must at all times be careful to approach cautiously, and get as near to the fish as possible without being observed. Many seem never to acquire the instinctive knowledge of the distance to keep from a trout without alarming it. The proficient has no difficulty in this respect; he sees at a glance the best way of manœuvring a pool or stream, although he may be a stranger to the river.

Further, the angler should always fish from the shallow or channel side, and disturb the water as little as possible if wading. If the whole stream is fishable, he commences at the foot of it; this is sometimes not practicable owing to the absence of wind, in which case his best plan is to strike the water's edge at the place where the ripple is first apparent. If he does not attend to this, he drives the fish up stream when walking along the edge, and alarms those lying above.

The attention of the angler ought in the first place to be directed to the shallow water next him, then with consecutive casts at varying angles let him methodically fish up the whole stream.

The greater proportion of casts are made upwards and across, but the channel side usually requires to be fished straight up stream. Each cast is made a little further up, and is spent where the preceding one began, the object of this being to keep the bait always moving in unfished water. The worm is allowed to come downward with the current in a natural way, and at the same time the rod top is slowly raised.

All sections of the stream, viz. the opposite bank, centre current, and shallow water, are in this way searched as the angler works his way upwards.

He should fish with special care all runs beneath the bank, the neighbourhood of large stones, tree roots, and places where the shallows merge into deeper water; while eddies and corners, of which there is great variety, must never be carelessly passed over, however shallow.

No time should be wasted when fishing small waters: but a large river is different; in it one stretch of good water for worm takes a long time to exhaust, and may sometimes, if broad enough, be fished over twice, the angler wading deeper on the second occasion.

Another favourite place for using worm is the "flatts," or thinnest description of water. These usually have a slight current running through them, which is every here and there diverted by large stones, or inequalities in the channel. If close to deep pools, this type of water often contains the best trout in the river. It is difficult to fish, a long line being necessary to keep the angler out of sight.

We have often found it an advantage both in streams and pools to complete each cast with a gentle draw downwards, the rod top being lowered somewhat before the sweep is given. By this means many a trout is secured that would otherwise have been merely touched. Fish often seize the worm as it is being lifted, which prevents the angler from striking effectively.

HOW TO FISH POOLS AND STILL WATER.— These portions of a river are rather uncertain; they require a good breeze, as we have already alluded to; with it, however, every place of moderate depth may be fished over, occasionally with great success. The angler must avoid very deep water, as in it sport is rarely obtained. The character of the water we speak of is unbroken, with or without current, and varying in depth from one to four or five feet. Tails of pools, mill-dams, stretches of flat water are embraced in it, and are to be met with in every river.

The angler may fish such places by throwing in his bait and allowing it to sink or travel slowly down stream, if there is any current. We, however, advise him to adopt another style of managing his line. It was first shown us several years ago by a professional angler, and on numerous occasions since we have proved its efficacy.

Casting upwards and across we allow the worm to rest a second, keeping a little more line than usual in the water; this is followed by giving the line a pull or sweep down or across the stream, lighter or stronger, according to the strength of the wind and depth of water; then resting the rod top a second, we complete the movement by another, but lighter draw down stream. The angler must always use his discretion as to the force necessary. In very shallow water the slightest touch will suffice, while in deeper places, disturbed by a strong wind, the first sweep should be of a bold character. Again, we have found this method very deadly on black windy days, usually considered the worst for worm-fishing. Weather of this description is more fitted for the minnow, and doubtless that lure would succeed better; but the worm makes a good substitute if correctly worked. It will be found that trout take it boldly, seldom missing their aim. In still water they usually look at the worm with great suspicion; we have, however, frequently seen them dash fearlessly at the bait when we accompanied the cast with a pull down stream.

Tails of pools are well suited for sport in this way when ruffled with wind. If calm the only portion of the pool that can be fished is the strong rush at the neck. This should be done in the same way as broken water, only fewer casts will exhaust it, and these should be made more directly up stream.

Catching rising fish in calm water affords capital practice. The angler must be able to throw a light line, and place his bait at the desired spot. Whenever a trout has risen he should cast a little above the place, and give his line the slightest pull towards the side or down stream. The smallest worms and thinnest wires, dressed on cobweb gut, are necessary for this description of fishing. If there is a breeze it is comparatively easy to catch rising fish, but in a dead calm it is extremely delicate work.

From the foregoing remarks it is evident that trout take a worm in still water with far greater boldness if there is imparted to it an artificial or unnatural motion. We may add that it is a good plan to place a small swivel on the casting-line; it causes the bait to spin slightly.

Some anglers fish only in the strong water at the necks of pools and streams; we do not recommend this, unless there happens to be a long stretch of river to cover. A fine average of trout may be taken in this way, but wherever the fishing-ground is limited, as in many of our rivers, we advise the angler to make the most of each stream and pool, without wasting time over the deep water.

FLOODED WATERS.—Our remarks up to this point have applied solely to rivers when at their summer level; we now turn to flooded waters.

In the first place, we advise anglers to be on the river when it is either rising or falling. During the height of a heavy flood very little sport is obtained, as trout seek refuge from the current under banks and stones, or retire to less disturbed quarters, where they lie until the water commences to subside. The angler should confine his operations to edges of pools, long stretches of unbroken water, and, in fact, every quiet corner.

Again, he need not cover much ground; if he knows a reliable spot where the trout are numerous, he should make for it, and stick to it.

As regards tackle, we have already recommended a good-sized single hook with larger worms; stronger gut should also be used, and sinkers consisting either of shot or lead wire.

All clear-water fishers exercise very little

patience when rivers are discoloured; it is contrary to their notions of sport; a spate, however, is useful in cleaning the bed of the stream, and stirs up large trout to feed more boldly.

Although it is when flooded that the banks of a river are most crowded, we can assure our readers it is no true criterion of the best time to fish; we have enjoyed good sport for a week or two when the river was small, disturbed only by an occasional angler. Whenever the rain came the whole neighbourhood turned out with rods, every one apparently thinking that the most favourable opportunity had arrived. On such days we have seldom found that good takes were general.

BURNS.—Burns are improved with a little extra water; when small they require to be fished with much of the skill necessary for the main stream. Light and accurate casting is of great importance, and it is necessary to fish more directly up stream. A shorter rod will be found better adapted for the narrow channel. Burn trout are never very fastidious, and generally take either fly or worm greedily; they afford good sport, but rarely equal in average or quality those met with in streams running through richer soil. The inducement to burn-fishing consists, to a great extent, in the invigorating hill air, fine scenery, and splendid exercise it affords.

CHAPTER IV.

MINNOW-FISHING.

MINNOW-FISHING is certainly one of the most fascinating methods of angling. Requiring a little less dexterity than fly-fishing, and somewhat less intimate knowledge of the haunts of trout than clear-water worm, it surpasses both in excitement. For it appeals to the appetites of the largest trout, and these fish, when pursuing a minnow, do so with a most wonderful mixture of caution and dash, following the lure until they imagine that it seems likely to escape, and then making such a rush at it as is apt to send the angler's heart into his mouth, and the minnow into theirs if allowed.

The rod which we prefer is an unsplit bamboo with greenheart top, moderately stiff, and of between 13 and 16 feet in length. We prefer a longish rod because it allows the minnow to be swung, not flopped into the water; besides, it gives greater command both over the spinning and hooking departments.

MINNOW-FISHING.

REEL.—This should be large and easy running, containing a fair quantity of line; the best for spinning is waterproofed silk, as it is less apt to kink than others. The line should taper sufficiently to allow the trace or casting-line to be affixed directly to it; and this trace should vary in length and fineness according to the state of the water when it is to be used. For thick or flooded water a trace a yard long, with two swivels, and composed of medium gut, is sufficient; but for clear, much-fished streams it should taper from thick trout gut, at the upper end, to the very finest undrawn gut of which the two or three strands next the hook should be composed, and be from 6 to 9 feet in length.

The best tackle, in our opinion, consists of a long-shanked body hook, with a smaller lip-hook;

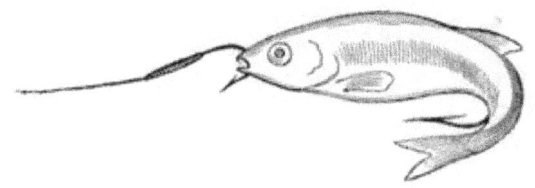

in spated water or large rivers a flying triangle may be found useful.

The size of the large hook should vary with that of the bait. (Nos. 1 and 2 of Messrs. Bartleet's round-bends are good general sizes.) The big hook should be of such length that from the top of the shank to the bend may equal the distance from the nose to the vent of the minnow.

We use a modification of this, consisting of a lip hook with swivel attached, and having a loop on the shank through which the gut between large hook and triangle is passed.

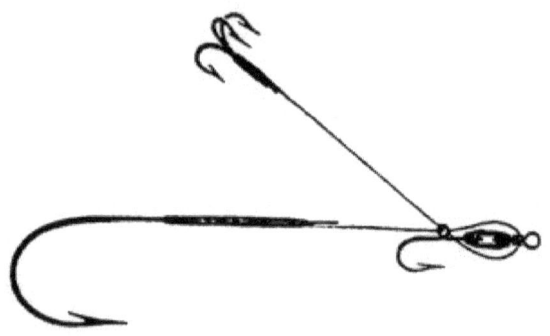

By easing the gut and drawing out either hook or triangle, this tackle can be made to suit any reasonable size of bait. Another good tackle is composed of a lip hook and two or three sets of double hooks so applied as to give the desired curve to the tail of the bait. As this can be obtained from any dealer, and the mode of baiting is quite simple, a diagram is unnecessary.

It must be noted that the object of all minnow tackle is twofold: first, to give a brilliant spin to the bait; secondly, to hook securely any fish that may dash at it.

To attain the former of these objects the tail of the bait must be well curved and the body perfectly straight. If the fore-part of the body is at all bent the result will be not a spin, but a wobble. Now a minnow when stunned does often spin, but it never wobbles. At the same time all fishes in swimming bend the tail from one side to the other, hence a curved bait is actually more natural than a straight one.

Our second object—secure hooking—is more likely to be attained by a single large hook with its point projecting at the tail (which, in our experience, is the part aimed at by trout), than by several smaller ones not in the right place. At the same time in coloured or large open waters fish often turn abruptly from the bait just when on the point of striking at it; hence the use of the flying triangle in such cases. Of artificial spinners and artificial baits we have but a poor opinion, the only artificial minnow with which we have done fairly well being the quill minnow, and next to this we would place a small Devon. Phantoms, though good in lochs, do not seem to have the ghost of a chance in rivers: this statement is a severe combination of joke and earnest.

TIMES AND SEASONS.—Fish take minnow best in the early part of the day; but often good fish seem to go minnow-hunting in the afternoon and late at night. The best hours are, however, at daybreak and nightfall, as these are the times when predatory animals of all sorts sally forth.

The time of year best for minnow is from June till the end of August, but a few fish may be taken with it at all times of the year, winter certainly not excepted.

Now for the application.

Fish on the lookout for minnows have a way of lying in wait in spots suited for their concealment, near shallows which their prey frequent; and thence rushing out and hunting down any unfortunate that seems at all disabled. It is, of course, impossible to mention all such places, but the likeliest of all are sudden depressions in the channel, the edges of deep eddies, the sides of large stones, tufts of grass and overhanging banks, and last, but not least, the roots of any tree that are washed by the current, or spaces amidst weeds.

These are good at all times, but in a porter-coloured water there is hardly a spot in any river fit to hold a trout where you may not spin successfully.

Now as to the method of spinning. Select a proper bait—the best are from $1\frac{1}{4}$ to $2\frac{1}{2}$ inches long—plump and clear (dark-coloured baits are little use): enter the large hook of the tackle, either at the mouth or gills of the bait—we prefer the former if we have a long-shanked hook, the latter if a short-shanked one—impale it till the point comes out near the tail, thus imparting the curve of the hook to the tail of the bait; pass the lip-hook through both lips, and there you are! A little care in this will be well repaid, as the main difficulty lies in getting the bend.

Now carefully approach the stream, and swing your bait first almost across the current, aiming it at a point a little above the water, thus allowing it to hang in the air a little before it descends; then, letting it sink slightly, draw the bait by a succession of pulls, with occasional pauses, slowly in a fast current, more quickly in a gentle one, *but never rapidly*, across and against the current, so that the minnow may spin in a curve athwart the stream. As your bait passes any likely spot you may expect a rush at it; but if not, never mind, simply go on spinning more and more carefully as it approaches the side, and then *edge* your minnow, searching thoroughly the shore, for we do not think we exaggerate in saying that two out of every three good trout taken by minnow seize the lure close to the side. When a fish takes the bait your strike must be firm and slow; in fact rather a continued strain than a jerk.

The great secret of success is to aim at imitating a sick, injured, or frightened minnow; therefore you must not spin continuously, nor drag the bait forcibly up stream, which no small fish could stem, but rather try to make your bait appear as if striving unsuccessfully against the current, and making for the friendly shelter of the margin.

This is the ordinary method of minnow-fishing, and that most successful in flooded waters and in large deep streams; but in small, clear waters the minnow should be cast more or less directly up stream and spun downwards. Many anglers will not believe that this is possible, but those who attempt it, after a little experience of the ordinary plan, will find it much easier than it sounds. The tactics here are precisely the same as those employed in the down-stream method *mutatis mutandis*, but the bait is best spun with a somewhat darting motion, so as to imitate the action of a frightened fish rushing down stream.

In both these plans it is sometimes necessary to weight the line, and this is accomplished either by a pear-shaped lead pushed into the bait's mouth, or better, by split shot applied *between* the two swivels.

In rivers frequented by salmon, parr-tail is often preferable to minnow[1] (or where parr are

---

[1] This is only legal on Tweed and its tributaries, and there not during April and May.

not available, the latter end of a small trout will do), and may be fished with in much stronger and deeper currents.

It is prepared by trimming off the fins and tail from a parr, and with a sharp knife cutting obliquely from the front of the anal to the front of the dorsal fin.

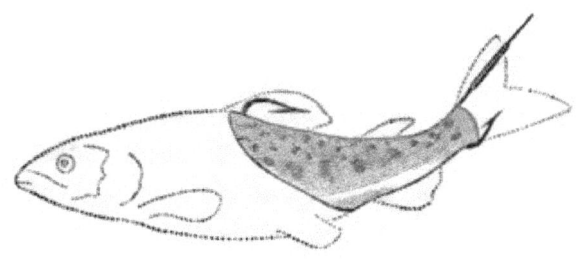

The lozenge-shaped bit of fish thus cut is used reversed, *i.e. like the brewer's horse, its tail where the head should be*, the large hook impaling it, and coming out near the farther end of the dorsal fin, whilst the lip hook pierces the gristle of the tail. This makes a very tough and lasting bait. It will sometimes be found an advantage to tie the end of the bait round the curve of the hook with thread; this preserves the parr-tail longer. The best size of parr for use is one from four to four and three-quarters inches long.

There are other ways of using minnow, which we may mention: Dead-minnow fishing, in which a fresh minnow is impaled by means of a baiting needle on a long-shanked bait hook heavily leaded, the needle being entered at the mouth, and brought out at the tail, so that the leaded shank of the hook is concealed in the belly, whilst the bend projects.

A better plan is to use a triangle with three or four split shot on the line above it. The tail is trimmed off or not according to taste, and a loop of the gut passed round the thin part to keep the bait straight. The minnow is then carefully dropped into any deep hole or eddy close to the side, and allowed to dart of its own weight to the bottom, or near it; then it is slowly drawn up a foot or so, and this process is continued until all the edges of the hole have been thoroughly searched. This plan is very deadly in hot sultry weather and during floods. It is a method well fitted for deep running, sluggish waters, with cavernous banks.

There is yet another way of using the minnow exactly like clear-water worm-fishing. In this method rippling streams only are fished, the smallest and brightest of minnows being impaled on a medium (No. 4 or 5) round-bend hook. A long rod and the finest of gut are necessary; the minnow is cast like a fly, and drawn gently down stream past all likely spots. The best time for this method is hot dry weather during July and

August, and it is sometimes specially good in the latter month.

We shall say nothing of live baiting, which we don't like, and don't care to use. It *may* be legitimate in rivers too sluggish for spinning, but, thank Heaven, we have none such in Scotland. Nor shall we say aught of trolling, which may sometimes be defensible in lochs, but should never be attempted on streams.

CHAPTER V.

CREEPER AND MAY-FLY FISHING.

We are aware that some ultra-fastidious fishers decry all baits, and look with special aversion on such lures as creeper, May-fly, cad-bait, etc. The best thing such persons can do is to skip this chapter altogether; they should certainly not try any of these baits lest they be converted.

Creeper and May-fly are the larval and complete stages of the same insect—the stone-fly of England, the May-fly and Gauger of Scotland, Perla Maxima and Perla Marginata of entomologists.

In any fast stream during the end of April and in May, on lifting a broad flat stone in shallow water, several ugly customers will be seen scuttling off, and perhaps one or two may be found adhering to the under surface of the stone. Examine one of them; it answers the popular description, "a rum 'un to look at—a beggar to go." The usual length is from three-fourths of an inch to one inch. A small venomous-looking head, three segments overlapping one another Inverness cape-wise for a chest, and a body or tail of nine or ten segments tapering slightly, terminated by two sting-like whisks, make its appearance somewhat formidable. Legs —yes, it has legs, only six of them, but they feel as if their name was legion, so rapidly do they move. Colour, mottled olive above; yellow below. Such is the creeper.

The fly is a big, soft, greenish-bodied fellow, from one to one and a quarter inches long, with four heavy, soft, drab-coloured wings, laid flat along its back.

Both are thoroughly harmless, until the angler renders them otherwise to the trout by inserting hooks.

The easiest way to catch creepers is to hire a small boy; if that useful nuisance is not available, a supply can be obtained by wading into a stream about six inches deep, holding a small-meshed landing-net below you, and displacing the stones with your feet. The slowest way is to lift stones and chase the insect; this is exciting but unprofitable. May-flies may be gathered from under stones near the water's edge, especially on the lee side of the stream.

TACKLE.—A long rod, somewhat soft in the top, is advisable, owing to the tender nature of both lures. Any kind of line, and a gut cast of from seven to nine feet long, ending in three or four strands of fine drawn gut, are to be used. The best tackle is made exactly like a small minnow tackle, *i.e.* one largish hook, say No. 9 or 10 Bartleet, and a smaller, No. 11 or 12 lip-hook, just above it. The larger hook may either be passed along the body, and so be hid by it, or it may be entered crosswise through it, whilst the smaller pierces the thorax or chest. A small single hook is often used, but we prefer the two hooks at all times and in all places. The tackle we have mentioned is suitable for either creeper or May-fly.

Split shot are generally advisable when using the creeper, both on account of the rapid nature of the water fished in, and to help in casting the bait, which is a small and light one in comparison to the rod by which it is thrown.

THE CREEPER.—The creeper comes on about the time that the March brown fly disappears, viz. the end of April, and continues till the end of May or beginning of June, when it turns into the May-fly. During the earlier parts of its season it is good only in the early morning, but further on it may be used continuously all day under suitable conditions. What are suitable conditions? Well, the water must be low and clear, the weather warm and bright, or if dull there must be a mild breeze; and trout require to be lying in the strong streams. The method of angling is precisely similar to that used in up-stream worm-fishing, quick striking being necessary, but a shorter line must be employed, owing to the softness of the bait.

The best places are rough strong currents full of boulders or rocks, and the greatest care should be taken in fishing the upper parts of all streams, as these are the spots where creepers do most abound. All streamy or broken water ought to be fished, but less attention should be given to *very* shallow places than is necessary in worm-fishing. The largest and clearest-coloured baits are best.

There is also an autumn creeper with which trout may be taken; it is, so far as we can see, but little different from the spring creeper; but we have not as yet satisfied ourselves as to the identity of its parent-fly.

CADDIS BAIT AND SCREW.—In this connection it may also be well to mention that caddis bait and the screw, or fresh-water shrimp, may be used in the same way as the creeper. The caddis, however, does better in pools than in streams. A good combination is to use caddis in the pools, creeper in the streams.

MAY-FLY.—The conditions most favourable to May-fly fishing are almost the exact opposite of those for creeper. A porter-coloured water, either during the rise or fall of a spate, is by far the best, and dull days, calm, or with a moderate breeze. Given such a day in May or June, and a good supply of bait, the angler may be happy yet.

The method is similar to that used for creeper-fishing; the tackle is baited in the same way, even the shot on the line being often useful in heavy streams, but greater care is necessary in casting, as the bait is very tender.

SHADE-FISHING.—The May-fly may also be used on very hot days to dape or shade fish with. That is to say, the angler stalks special fish in the pools, taking advantage of the shelter of trees and bushes to approach. The line is wound round the end of the rod and uncoiled until just sufficient line has been let out to allow the fly to paddle about on the top of the water, as near as possible to the intended victims' haunt: very large trout are sometimes taken in this way by those anglers who have patience for such proceedings.

CHAPTER VI.

LOCH-FISHING.

ALTHOUGH loch-fishing does not require the same amount of skill as river-fishing, it is still a most enjoyable pastime, the great attraction being the superior size of trout to be caught. The best rod in our opinion for fishing from a boat is one of 11 or 12 feet in length, light, stiffish, and which can easily be used with either hand. Should the angler intend fishing from the shore, his rod is better to be 12 to 14 feet long, as he often requires to cast further than is necessary while angling from a boat. The wood we recommend for a rod of this description is greenheart entirely, or bamboo cane with a top piece of hickory and lance-wood. The best line is one of silk and hair, or waterproof silk, the latter, for choice, of a yellowish brown colour, and 40 or 50 yards in length. It is always advisable to have the line tapered off with 3 feet of twisted gut; this should be spliced to the line so that it may not catch on the rings of the rod while being reeled in.

Next comes a most important part of the outfit, the reel, which should balance the rod. The best reel is an easy-going ratchet, with the spring just sufficiently strong to prevent the line over-running. Most ratchets are much too stiff, and if a heavy fish is hooked on fine tackle with one of these, it is almost a hopeless case; there are probably more fish and tackle lost by a stiff-running reel than by any other cause the loch angler has to contend with.

The fishing-book should consist of two parts, the one composed of large pockets for made-up casting-lines, and the other constructed in the ordinary manner for holding flies.

A landing-net is a necessity while angling from a boat. It should be 2 feet deep, the circumference of the ring $3\frac{1}{2}$ feet, and the handle 4 feet long.

Of casting, which has already been described in the chapter on river-fishing, we shall say little, simply noting that it is necessary to cast in the same direction as the boat is drifting, viz. with the wind. It should be borne in mind that it is much better to cast lightly and straight, 6 or 8 yards (which in most cases from a boat is quite sufficient) than 12 or 14 yards, that go down on the water zig-zag, leaving the line so loose that a fish rising cannot be hooked. If there be only one angler fishing from a boat he should try and cover as much water as possible by casting first to the right, then straight forward, and then to the left.

The casting-line should be from 8 to 10 feet long, and attached to the line by a loop, the flies being put on as described in the chapter on tackle.

The number and size of flies to be used must be ruled entirely by the state of the water and weather.

If it is very calm two small river flies, 3 feet apart, should be used on a casting-line of the finest undrawn gut. If there is a fair ripple on the water use three flies, 3 feet apart, Nos. 9 or 10 (in April and May a size larger may be required). Again, if the waves are of a moderate size, four flies, never more, 2 feet apart, may be used, Nos. 7 or 8. The above numbers are W. Bartleet & Son's Kendal round-bends.

For angling in northern lochs such as Tay, Vennacher, Earn, Awe, etc., these flies are at least a size too small. We think, however, that many anglers make the mistake of using too large flies, more especially on artificial lochs, which as a rule require flies of a small size. In bright weather dull-coloured flies should be used; and in cloudy weather, or in peaty water, brighter flies, with tinsel on the body, are best.

One of the most important things to be learned is the different manner in which the fly should be worked in varying circumstances, and this can only be found out by experience; but we shall try to explain the modes we approve of.

When the breeze is light, trout generally rise best if the flies are drawn slowly and directly against the ripple. When we say slowly, we mean just sufficiently fast to keep the flies on the surface of the water. If the waves are fairly large and choppy, the flies should be drawn slowly sideways between them. Again, if there is more of a swell than a wave, it is advisable to let the flies sink slightly, and draw them sideways. There are, however, exceptions to every rule, so that the various ways should be tried alternately until a fish is taken. In very stormy weather it often happens that the only place to get fish with fly is immediately in the lee of the boat, where the surface is more or less sheltered from the wind.

In angling from the shore, if the breeze is light, the angler will require to cast frequently, and draw the flies towards the edge. If there is a good breeze, the flies should be allowed to drift for about 3 feet, and then be drawn slowly inwards. To avoid fishing over the same water twice, a step should be taken after each cast. Angling from the shore is in many respects like river-fishing, as the trout lie beneath trees, near reeds, boulders, etc.; and these places must be carefully fished.

The next subject is one on which there are great differences of opinion—" When and how to strike : " this we think depends greatly on the state of the water, and how the fish are rising. Striking should be done entirely by the wrist being brought up sharply but gently in the direction of the shoulder, without moving the arm.

On a calm day, when the fish are rising shyly, we believe in striking immediately the surface of the water is broken. If the fish are rolling over the fly, porpoise fashion, the strike should be delayed until the fish has turned. Again, if the fish are rising out of the water and taking the fly on the downward course, the line should be kept taut, and the fish allowed to hook themselves.

More than half the battle in loch-angling is knowing the ground on which the feeding fish lie. Unless this is known the best plan is for the boatman to row very slowly and quietly against the wind, whilst the angler, with a long line, casts at right angles from the stern of the boat. Should he get a rise, or see fish rising, let the boatman row on about 100 yards, and then turn and drift as nearly as possible over the spot on which the fish were seen feeding. If he finds that this manœuvre succeeds, let him take several short drifts about the same place until the take comes to an end. There is no doubt that in many lochs the fish go in shoals, so that the angler should be in no hurry to leave the spot on which the fish are feeding on the supposition that he would do better elsewhere. Beginners frequently change too often from one drift to another, and, owing to this, probably miss the take when it is on.

As to the various depths of water to be fished during the season, the following general rule will be found useful:—March, April, and September 6 to 8 feet; May and June 4 to 8 feet; July and August 3 to 6 feet.

An easy way to find the depths is to sound occasionally with an oar. In such lochs as Tay and Earn the only fishing-ground is near the shore, so that the angler must be careful not to let the boat drift into too deep water.

When playing a fish the rod should be kept almost perpendicular, and the line never allowed to get slack except in the case of a leap out of the water, when the point of the rod should momentarily be lowered. One thing to be done immediately a large fish is hooked is to try and take it to windward. If this is not attended to in stormy weather, the boat is almost certain to drift over the line and entangle the flies. Great care must be taken when using the landing-net to sink it well, and whenever the fish is seen to be safely within it, the point of the rod should be lowered.

LOCH-FISHING.

The day on which sport may be looked for with the greatest certainty on most lochs is one with a gentle south-westerly breeze, a dull sky and occasional showers. Probably the most unfavourable day is one with a cloudless sky and no wind. Between these extremes there are states of weather in which the take appears to depend on the caprice of the trout. On Lochleven, which in some respects is a rule unto itself, the best sport is had when there is a steady easterly breeze accompanied by a drizzling rain.

Trolling with fly is sometimes practised with success. This is done by letting out 35 or 40 yards of line from the stern, and having the boat rowed very slowly and quietly. The flies should be a size larger than would otherwise be used, and the gut stouter to meet the extra strain.

The following is a list of flies which we have proved to be successful in a variety of lochs :—

    Teal wing, with red, green, yellow, or blue body.
    Mallard wing, with red or black body.
    Woodcock wing, with hare-lug, red, or yellow body.
    Blae wing, with black or water-rat body.
    Grouse wing, with red, green, or orange body.
    March brown.
    Hecham Pecham, with red, yellow, or green body.
    Corncrake wing, with yellow, or dark orange body.
    Bustard wing, with red or yellow body.
    Black Palmer, with red tip (Zulu).
    Claret hackle, orange body and yellow tip.

Trolling with minnow is often successful, although we do not advise its use, unless the fish cannot be taken with fly. The rod should be 14 or 15 feet in length, and built entirely of greenheart. The best line is waterproofed silk, and it should be at least 100 yards long. It is advisable to have it marked off at various lengths with a few turns of different coloured threads varnished over; for instance, red at 30 yards, white at 40 yards, blue at 50 yards.

It is necessary to find out at what depth the fish are feeding, and this can only be done by letting out various lengths of line from 30 to 50 yards. Thus, if a fish is taken when the line is out to the extent of the white thread (40 yards), let the line again out to the same length, and so on. In trolling with minnow the boat should be rowed zig-zag and rather faster than when trolling with fly. The artificial minnows most deadly are the phantom and angel, the former if the loch is shallow, and the latter if deep. Regarding size and colour we prefer the blue and silver or brown and gold phantom of about $1\frac{1}{2}$ inches in length; the best angel is one entirely white, or brown and white, and of the same size as the former. Natural minnow is sometimes very deadly, and should be used on a two-hook tackle, as described in the chapter on minnow-fishing. There are numerous kinds of minnow tackles, but the above will be found the best and simplest. The trace or casting-line should have two or three swivels, and be made of stouter gut than would be used in river-fishing.

Trolling is occasionally successful on a calm day with bright sunshine, but, as a rule, the best sport is obtained when a boisterous wind is blowing.

There still remains another branch in loch-fishing, and that is angling from the shore with worm, which in very bright or very stormy weather occasionally does fairly well; we only recommend its use, however, when all other resources fail. Large worms should be used on a single bait-hook, of which there may be two on the casting-line—one about $2\frac{1}{2}$ feet above the other, and put on in the same manner as a fly. The best places are near burn mouths, if they are flooded, or where the water deepens rapidly. As long a line as possible must be cast, and the bait allowed to sink to the bottom: this done, the line should be drawn slowly, in very short jerks, towards the shore. Should a fish bite the line is allowed to rest a moment until it is again felt, when the angler should strike.

CHAPTER VII.

SOME HINTS AS TO TACKLE.

The angler's equipment having been touched upon in each of the preceding chapters, we have only to add a few hints regarding it.

Gut.—The finest undrawn is difficult to procure, and for that reason drawn gut is now largely employed. The latter is strong enough when carefully handled to land large trout, but more skill is required to cast it properly.

If the angler makes up his own tackle he should be provided with two hanks of gut, drawn and undrawn; with these he can vary his casts during the season to suit all weathers.

Various dyes may be employed to stain gut. An infusion of logwood, with the addition of a very minute piece of copperas, gives a bluish colour. If afterwards steeped in strong warm tea the gut takes on a duller shade, and loses much of its glitter. Copperas must always be used sparingly, otherwise it rots the gut. Unless the angler is accustomed to dye gut, he is safer to purchase it stained the colour he wishes.

To preserve gut, it should be wrapped in chamois skin, or any soft, close material: when exposed to the light for any time it becomes brittle.

Before making up a cast, steep the gut in warm water, then lay the ends of two strands side by side, form a loop, pass the gut through it, and draw tight.

SINGLE WATER KNOT.

The diagram shows the single knot; the double knot is made by passing the ends through twice.

The "Fisherman's Knot" is also well known; hold the gut as before, with the short ends make half hitches round the line, either single or double, draw them tight, and pull together.

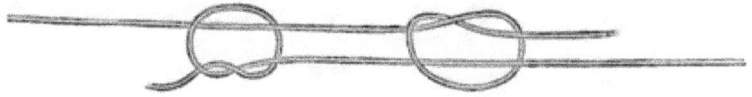

SINGLE FISHERMAN'S KNOT.

Where single knots are used, the waste ends should not be cut away too close.

Various methods are employed to fix on droppers : we give a few of them :—

1st. Lay dropper parallel with casting-line, above a knot, fly pointing *upwards*, make a double half-hitch round the cast with gut end of dropper, and pull tight.

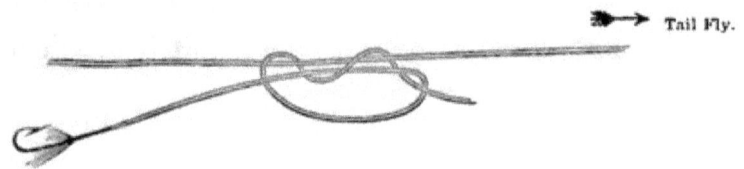

2d. Tie on dropper to cast with a single knot, draw it tight, then, pointing fly downward, make a hitch round the line, and pull upwards. This also requires to be placed above a knot on the cast.

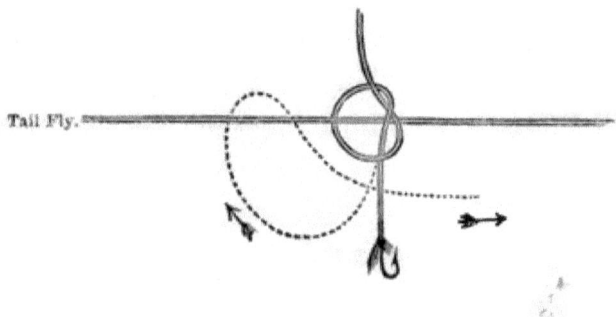

3d. Make a running loop on cast, insert gut of dropper, and with slight jerk draw both ends of casting-line in opposite directions. It will then be found that the dropper is quite secure. Both fly and casting-line require to be well soaked for this attachment.

4*th*. The gut of droppers may be used to form part of the main line, as the diagram will explain. This is a neat and secure way of making up the cast, but care should be taken that the gut of dropper (*a*) and casting-line are of the same thickness.

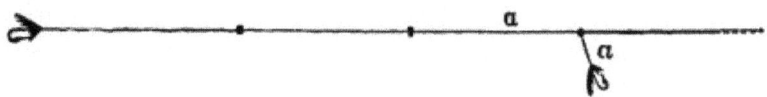

The gut cast may be attached to the reel-line in the following way.

After a day's fishing the wet portion of the line should be unwound and dried. To prevent ravelling it should be coiled round the back of a chair or flat piece of wood, or a winder made for the purpose may be used.

Reels, more especially those with revolving plates, are easily injured; the anglers must therefore be careful to prevent them coming in contact with any hard substance, and must also avoid laying them down near sand. If the plate does not run smoothly it should be unscrewed and well cleaned.

Rods, either when mounted or in their covers, ought never to be placed against a wall, as they are apt to warp.

The rod cover should always be kept dry, and it is therefore better to carry it about as little as possible.

To prevent the joints of the rod slipping it is safer to tie them together with waxed thread, small catches being usually lapped on the rod for this purpose.

As breakages may occur, the angler should never go a-fishing without some well-waxed cord or narrow linen tape.

A strong knife is indispensable, and a pair of folding scissors will also be found useful.

Wading boots and waterproof fishing-stockings require looking after, the former to be oiled, and the latter turned inside out after use to allow all dampness to escape, and then re-turned.

It is sometimes necessary to carry a landing-net. We prefer one with solid metal ring, of moderate depth, and with a handle from 3 to $3\frac{1}{2}$ feet in length. For loch-fishing a larger size is necessary.

CHAPTER VIII.

THE LAW OF SCOTLAND AS TO TROUT-FISHING.

It must be admitted that a legal disquisition seems somewhat out of place in a book devoted to sport, but the rights and grievances of anglers have of late received so much attention that a brief statement of the law relating to trout-fishing may prove both interesting and useful. As this chapter is not written for members of the legal profession, the simplest possible language will be used, and the pages will not be cumbered with references to authorities. To prevent confusion it may be well to state at the outset that we only propose to deal with the law of Scotland, and that what we have to say does not apply to salmon-fishing.

In what are termed public navigable rivers, trout may be captured by every one; and—this is, however, not so certain—it is thought that the same rule applies to lochs "forming great channels of communication in a district of country." In exercising this right, however, the banks of the stream beyond high-water mark, or the shores of the loch, where either of these are private property, must not be trespassed upon. A public navigable river may be defined in this connection as "one which is fit for the transportation of the country products;" but an opinion is expressed by the leading authority on Scotch fishery law that the right of angling is confined to that portion of the river which is within the influence of the tide.

It has long been decided that the right of trout-fishing in private rivers—that is, in all rivers which do not fall within the category we have just considered—passes as a pertinent of the adjoining land. Put into plain English, this means that the proprietor of every piece of ground intersected or bounded by a stream has, without the necessity of any written grant, the privilege of angling for trout in that stream, in so far as it washes his estate. If he possess the ground on both sides, he is entitled to fish the whole breadth of the river; if, on the other hand, only one of the banks should belong to him, his boundary, beyond which he may not wade, is an imaginary line drawn down the centre of the stream. Some authorities hold that in the latter case he cannot even throw his line into his neighbour's half of the water; but this has not been decided by the Scotch Courts, and seems open to question.

It has been laid down by the Court of Session that no one has any right to angle in a private river without the consent of the proprietor; that such a right cannot be inferred from the fact that members of the public have actually fished a particular piece of water without let or hindrance for any length of time; that even where there is a right of way by the riverside, fishing from the road or path can be prevented by the proprietor; and several judges have expressed the opinion that a tenant has no right to fish in a river or loch upon his farm without the consent of his landlord. These decisions show that it is only at the pleasure of the lairds that a line can be thrown upon any private river throughout the length and breadth of Scotland.

The rules as to fishing in private lochs are slightly different from those which apply to rivers. Where a loch is situated wholly within one estate, then, as before, the proprietor has the exclusive right. When it is bounded by different properties, however, and the matter is not regulated by the respective titles, each landowner can fish over the whole loch; but in doing so he must not trespass upon his neighbour's ground. Following up this principle, it was decided that a proprietor on the shores of Loch Rannoch was entitled to confer on a purchaser of a portion of his estate all the privileges he himself enjoyed, including that of angling. This decision, followed to its logical conclusion, would seem to confer on the owner of a small strip of ground on the margin of any of our inland seas the power to multiply indefinitely the number of persons entitled to fish in its waters; but some of the judges indicated that if a case of this kind were to arise the court might interfere to protect the interests of the other proprietors. This, however, being mere expression of opinion, has not the authority of a formal judgment.

Although the landowners have, as we have seen, the exclusive right of fishing in private rivers and lochs, they have no right of property in the fish themselves. To use the legal term, trout are *ferae naturae*, and the rule is that so long as they retain their natural liberty they belong to no one. The practical result of this is that an angler who has captured trout by rod and line is entitled to retain them, even although he may have been fishing without permission.

A proprietor who finds any one angling in his water is entitled to order the offender off, and, if necessary, to use force to compel him to leave. It must be kept in view, however, that if more violence is employed than the occasion requires, there may be a claim for damages. If any one fish in the knowledge that the proprietor objects, and still more if, after being warned off, he persist in returning, the remedy is to raise an action of interdict. If the suit be successful, the defender will generally be ordered to pay the costs; and disregard of the interdict, when granted, will be treated as contempt of court, and punished by fine or imprisonment.

Even the most careful angler may occasionally find himself unwittingly fishing in forbidden waters. In such a case the proper course is at once to apologise, and explain that the trespass was unintentional, and leave the river. It is probable that under these circumstances an application for interdict would only succeed if there were reason to doubt the *bona fides* of the explanation.

So much as to questions of right between proprietors and the public: we have still to consider what modes of fishing are legal and what illegal. Until the passing of the Acts after referred to, trout could be taken by any means which neither interfered unnecessarily with the salmon-fishing, if it belonged to a separate person, nor injured the trout-fishing of the neighbouring proprietors. But to prevent certain unsportsmanlike practices which were only too common, Parliament stepped in, and passed two Acts, one in the year 1845, and the other in 1860. By the second of these Acts, which is practically an extended edition of the first, it is declared illegal for any one, not being the proprietor of a fishing, or having his permission, " to fish for trout or other fresh-water fish in any river, water, or loch in Scotland, with any net of any kind or description, or by what is known as double-rod fishing, or cross-line fishing, or set lines, or otter fishing, or burning the water, or by striking the fish with any instrument, or by pointing, or to put into the water lime or any other substance destructive to trout or other fresh-water fish with intent to destroy the same." This list of offences seems wide enough to prohibit the capture of trout in any way except by means of rod and line, or by the more primitive, but, to some people, the equally enjoyable process of " guddling."

It has to be kept in view that these Acts only apply to persons who have no right to the fishing. A proprietor is thus, so far as their provisions are concerned, in the same position as before 1845 ; and cannot be challenged unless he act in such a way as to interfere with the neighbouring fisheries. Under this last principle such operations as the erection of weirs, or the introduction of poisonous or polluting matter into the water, may be prevented. There are Acts of Parliament dealing with pollution, but this is too large a subject to be entered upon here.

Two points in the Salmon Acts must be kept in view by all trout-fishers who wish to avoid getting into trouble. The first of these is the enactment which declares it to be illegal to use any fish roe as a bait, or even to possess it without a satisfactory reason; and the other is the prohibition of the capture of parr or smolts, or, broadly speaking, the young of any migratory fish of the salmon kind. This latter provision is only in force, so far as the Tweed and tributaries are concerned, during the months of April and May, but throughout the rest of the country it is operative all the year round.

We cannot conclude without calling attention to what is undoubtedly a grievous blot on the law of Scotland as regards trout-fishing,—the want, namely, of a close time. In these days, when the gradual depopulation of our streams is universally admitted and deplored, it is not very creditable that this simple reform should have been so long delayed. How urgently it is called for must be known to every one who is in the habit of visiting any of the stretches of open water throughout the country. During the spawning season large numbers of fish, quite unfit either for food or sport, are annually slaughtered; and it is impossible to estimate the extent to which the stock for ensuing years is thus diminished. We earnestly hope that ere long the trout **may** enjoy the brief **period** of protection which has been provided for so many other wild animals.

THE END.

Printed by T. and A. Constable, Printers to Her Majesty, at the Edinburgh University Press.

AMERICAN AUTHORS.

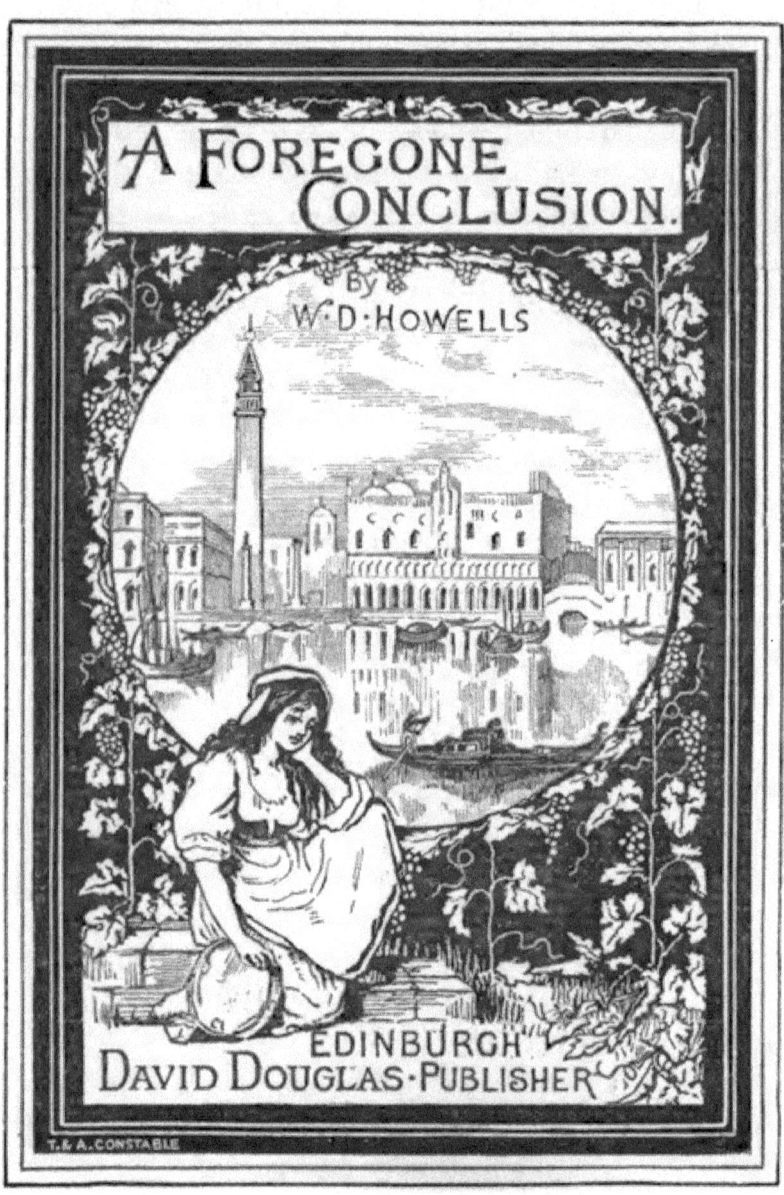

AMERICAN AUTHORS.

Latest Editions. Revised by the Authors. In 1s. volumes.
By Post, 1s. 2d.

Printed by Constable, and published with the sanction of the Authors.

By W. D. HOWELLS.
A Foregone Conclusion.
A Chance Acquaintance.
Their Wedding Journey.
A Counterfeit Presentment.
The Lady of the Aroostook. 2 vols.
Out of the Question.
The Undiscovered Country. 2 vols.
A Fearful Responsibility.
Venetian Life. 2 vols.
Italian Journeys. 2 vols.
The Rise of Silas Lapham. 2 vols.
Indian Summer. 2 vols.

By FRANK R. STOCKTON.
Rudder Grange.
The Lady or the Tiger?
A Borrowed Month.

By GEORGE W. CURTIS.
Prue and I.

By J. C. HARRIS (*Uncle Remus*).
Mingo, and other Sketches.

By GEO. W. CABLE.
Old Creole Days.
Madame Delphine.

By B. W. HOWARD.
One Summer.

By JOHN BURROUGHS.
Winter Sunshine.
Pepacton.
Locusts and Wild Honey.
Wake-Robin.
Birds and Poets.
Fresh Fields.

By OLIVER WENDELL HOLMES.
The Autocrat of the Breakfast Table. 2 vols.
The Poet. 2 vols.
The Professor. 2 vols.

By C. P. LATHROP.
An Echo of Passion.

By R. C. WHITE.
Mr. Washington Adams.

By T. B. ALDRICH.
The Queen of Sheba.
Marjorie Daw.
Prudence Palfrey.
The Stillwater Tragedy. 2 vols.

By B. MATTHEWS and H. C. BUNNER.
In Partnership.

By WILLIAM WINTER.
Shakespeare's England.
Wanderers: A Collection of Poems.

*** *Other Volumes of this attractive Series in preparation.*

Any of the above may be had bound in Cloth extra, at 2s. each volume.

'A set of charming little books.'—*Blackwood's Magazine.*
'A remarkably pretty series.'—*Saturday Review.*
'These neat and minute volumes are creditable alike to printer and publisher.'—*Pall Mall Gazette.*
'The most graceful and delicious little volumes with which we are acquainted.'—*Freeman.*
'Soundly and tastefully bound . . . a little model of typography, . . . and the contents are worthy of the dress.'—*St. James's Gazette.*
'The delightful shilling series of "American Authors" introduced by Mr. David Douglas, has afforded pleasure to thousands of persons.'—*Figaro.*
'The type is delightfully legible, and the page is pleasant for the eye to rest upon; even in these days of cheap editions we have seen nothing that has pleased us so well.'—*Literary World.*

EDINBURGH: DAVID DOUGLAS.

SCOTTISH STORIES AND SKETCHES.

Johnny Gibb of Gushetneuk in the Parish of Pyketillim, with Glimpses of Parish Politics about A.D. 1843. Ninth Edition, with Glossary, Fcap. 8vo, 2s.

Seventh Edition, with Twenty Illustrations—Portraits and Landscapes—by GEORGE REID, R.S.A. Demy 8vo, 12s. 6d.

'A most vigorous and truthful delineation of local character, drawn from a portion of the country where that character is peculiarly worthy of careful study and record.'—*The Right Hon. W. E. Gladstone.*

'It is a grand addition to our pure Scottish dialect; . . . it is not merely a capital specimen of genuine Scottish northern *dialect;* but it is a capital specimen of pawky characteristic Scottish humour. It is full of good hard Scottish dry fun.'—*Dean Ramsay.*

Life among my Ain Folk, by the Author of 'JOHNNY GIBB OF GUSHETNEUK.'

Contents.

1. Mary Malcolmson's Wee Maggie.
2. Couper Sandy.
3. Francie Herriegerie's Sharger Laddie.
4. Baubie Huie's Bastard Geet.
5. Glengillodram.

Fcap. 8vo. Second Edition. Cloth, 2s. 6d. Paper, 2s.

'Mr. Alexander thoroughly understands the position of men and women who are too often treated with neglect, and graphically depicts their virtues and vices, and shows to his readers difficulties, struggles, and needs which they are sure to be the wiser for taking into view.'—*Freeman.*

'"Baubie Huie's Bastard Geet," which is full of quiet but effective humour, is the clearest revelation we have ever seen of the feeling in Scotch country districts in regard to certain aspects of morality.'—*Spectator.*

'We find it difficult to express the warm feelings of admiration with which we have read the present volume.'—*Aberdeen Journal.*

'Done with a skilful and loving hand.'—*Daily Review.*

Notes and Sketches of Northern Rural Life in the Eighteenth Century, by the Author of 'JOHNNY GIBB OF GUSHETNEUK.' In 1 vol. Fcap. 8vo, 2s. and 1s.

'This delightful little volume. It is a treasure. . . . We admire the telling simplicity of the style, the sly, pawky, Aberdonian humour, the wide acquaintance with the social and other conditions of the northern rural counties of last century, and the fund of illustrative anecdotes which enrich the volume. The author has done great service to the cause of history and of progress. It is worth a great many folios of the old dry-as-dust type.'—*Daily Review.*

Scotch Folk. Illustrated. Third Edition enlarged. Fcap. 8vo, price 1s.

'They are stories of the best type, quite equal in the main to the average of Dean Ramsay's well-known collection.'—*Aberdeen Free Press.*

Rosetty Ends, or the Chronicles of a Country Cobbler. By Job Bradawl (A. DEWAR WILLOCK), Author of 'She Noddit to me.' Fcap. 8vo, Illustrated. 2s. and 1s.

'The sketches are amusing productions, narrating comical incidents, connected by a thread of common character running through them all—a thread waxed into occasional strength by the "roset" of a homely, entertaining wit.'—*Scotsman.*

EDINBURGH: DAVID DOUGLAS.

OPEN-AIR BOOKS.

How to Catch Trout. By THREE ANGLERS. Illustrated, 1s.
'The aim of this little book is to give, within the smallest space possible, such practical information and advice as will enable the beginner, without further instruction, to attain moderate proficiency in the use of every legitimate lure.'

On Horse-breaking. By ROBERT MORETON. Second Edition, 1s.

A Year in the Fields. By JOHN WATSON. Fcap. 8vo, 1s.
'A charming little work. A lover of life in the open air will read the book with unqualified pleasure.'—*Scotsman.*

May in Anjou, with other Sketches and Studies. By ELEANOR C. PRICE, Author of 'A Lost Battle,' etc. Fcap. 8vo, 1s.

Iona. With Illustrations. By the DUKE OF ARGYLL. Fcap. 8vo, 1s.

Studies of Great Cities—Paris. By D. BALSILLIE, M.A. Fcap. 8vo, 1s.
'The charm of Mr. Balsillie's "Studies" is that they are personal reminiscences of things seen, and the personal element enters largely into the description. They are brightly-written conversational sketches of the scenes that meet the eye of the visitor to Paris—the streets, the picture-galleries, Versailles, and Notre Dame. All are entertaining, and a man must know his Paris very thoroughly who finds nothing to learn from them.'—*Scotsman.*

On the Links; being Golfing Stories by various hands, with 'Shakespeare on Golf.' By a NOVICE. Also two Rhymes on Golf by ANDREW LANG. Fcap. 8vo, 1s.

The Art of Golf. By Sir W. G. SIMPSON, Bart. In 1 vol. demy 8vo, with twenty plates from instantaneous photographs of Professional Players, chiefly by A. F. Macfie, Esq. Price 15s.
'He has devoted himself for years with exemplary zeal to the collecting of everything which a true golfer would like to know about the royal game, and the result of his labour is worthy of the highest commendation. . . . The prominent feature of the volume is the set of Illustrations. For the first time, by means of instantaneous photography, are produced on paper the movements made by players, with a classical style in the process of striking a golf ball.'—*Scotsman.*

The Gamekeeper's Manual; being an Epitome of the Game Laws of England and Scotland, and of the Gun Licences and Wild Birds Acts. By ALEXANDER PORTER, Chief Constable of Roxburghshire. Second edition, crown 8vo, 3s.
'A concise and valuable epitome to the Game Laws, specially addressed to those engaged in protecting game.'—*Scotsman.*
'An excellent and compactly written little handbook.'—*Free Press*, Aberdeen.

Modern Horsemanship: A New Method of Teaching Riding and Training by means of Instantaneous Photographs from the Life. By E. L. ANDERSON. Third edition, with fresh illustrations of 'The Gallop-Change,' of unique and peculiar interest. In 1 vol. demy 8vo. Illustrated. Price 21s.
'The best new English work on riding and training that we can recommend is the book "Modern Horsemanship."'—*The Sport Zeitung*, Vienna.
'Every page shows the author to be a complete master of his subject.'—*The Field.*

EDINBURGH: DAVID DOUGLAS.

LITTLE BROWN BOOKS.

Foolscap 8vo, Sixpence each.

The Religion of Humanity: An Address delivered at the Church Congress, Manchester, October 1888, by the Right Hon. ARTHUR J. BALFOUR, M.P., LL.D., etc., 6d.

'We have called the pamphlet a sermon because it is one, though the fitting text, "The fool hath said in his heart, There is no God," is courteously omitted; and we venture to say that of all who will read it, not one per cent. ever read or heard one more convincing or intellectually more delightful.'—*Spectator.*

[A large type edition of this may also be had in cloth at 5s.]

Fishin' Jimmy, by A. T. SLOSSON. 6d. '*A choice story from America.*'

'A story from which, in its simplicity and pathos, we may all learn lessons of wisdom and charity.'—*Freeman.*

'A pathetic but pretty little story, telling the simple life of one possessed of a profound veneration for all things heavenly, yet viewing them with the fearless questioning eyes of the child.'—*Literary World.*

'Macs' in Galloway. By PATRICK DUDGEON. 6d.

Rab and his Friends. By Dr. JOHN BROWN. 6d.

Marjorie Fleming. By Dr. JOHN BROWN. 6d.

Our Dogs. By Dr. JOHN BROWN. 6d.

'With Brains, Sir.' By Dr. JOHN BROWN. 6d.

Minchmoor. By Dr. JOHN BROWN. 6d.

Jeems the Door-Keeper. By Dr. JOHN BROWN. 6d.

The Enterkin. By Dr. JOHN BROWN. 6d.

Plain Words on Health. By Dr. JOHN BROWN. 6d.

Something about a Well: with more of Our Dogs. By Dr. JOHN BROWN. 6d.

WORKS BY DR. JOHN BROWN.

Horæ Subsecivæ. 3 Vols. 22s. 6d.

Vol. I. Locke and Sydenham. Fifth Edition, with Portrait by James Faed. Crown 8vo, 7s. 6d.

Vol. II. Rab and his Friends. Thirteenth Edition. Crown 8vo, 7s. 6d.

Vol. III. John Leech. Fifth Edition, with Portrait by George Reid, R.S.A. Crown 8vo, 7s. 6d.

Rab and his Friends. With India-proof Portrait of the Author after Faed, and seven Illustrations after Sir G. Harvey, Sir Noel Paton, Mrs. Blackburn, and G. Reid, R.S.A. Demy 4to, cloth, 9s.

Marjorie Fleming: A Sketch. Being a Paper entitled 'Pet Marjorie; A Story of a Child's Life fifty years ago.' New Edition, with Illustrations by Warwick Brookes. Demy 4to, 7s. 6d. and 6s.

Rab and his Friends. Cheap Illustrated Edition. Square 12mo ornamental wrapper, 1s.

EDINBURGH: DAVID DOUGLAS.

www.ingramcontent.com/pod-product-compliance
Lightning Source LLC
Chambersburg PA
CBHW032239080426
42735CB00008B/924